writing memoir

A Book of Writing Prompts

the san francisco writers' grotto
authors of *642 Things to Write About*

foreword by Julie Lythcott-Haims

ABRAMS NOTERIE, NEW YORK

writing memoir

Memoirists take on the risks associated with telling truths in public, and thus are the bug lighters of the literary world. Critics love to pick on us—they equate the genre to a gathering of nudists whose bodies no one wants to see. Family and friends can be critics, too—they may not like the secrets being revealed or the way they've been depicted on the page. (A worthy retort, satisfying in the moment: "If you didn't want to be in the book, you should've been nicer.") But whether memoirists are lauded as heroes or reviled as knaves is beside the point. The truth is worth telling. And sometimes the truth hurts.

But let's rewind. First, let's establish a definition for what memoir is. To me, *memoir is a true account of some aspect of one's life.* It is not autobiography, which is generally reserved for humans who know during their lifetimes that they are destined to become historical figures. Both forms aim to tell the truth of things as remembered by the subject, and both are vulnerable to accusations that the narrative veered toward make-believe or covered a subject not worthy of another human's time. But they differ in their scope. A memoir covers a particular experience, memorable period, or lesson learned; an autobiography tells a person's entire life. A person can write only one autobiography but can write innumerable memoirs. (A recent headline accompanying the publication of her third memoir screamed, "Joyce Maynard is still oversharing.")

It's also worthwhile to compare memoir to its sister, the novel. Whereas in a novel the reader is aware of three distinct points of view—the author who writes the book, the perspective from which the story is told, and the main character or protagonist who lives the story—in memoir, the author, narrator, and protagonist are one and the same. This requires a bit of psychological sorting, and embedded in the complexity is a critical lesson: A memoirist's central preoccupation is determining what the self knew (and when) and how the narrator should reveal the protagonist's journey to the reader, while doing a delicate dance with the changing nature of memory.

Unlike novelists, memoirists choose not to invent a world where anything goes and where the author will have complete deniability. Our oath is to the truth. Yet truth is not as ironclad a concept as it may seem. Think of it as fact versus perception; this seems like a clear distinction, yet is my perception not the pencil that records the facts of my life?

Following Thanksgiving dinner, for example, were you to ask all of your relatives to spend half an hour writing down what happened during the meal, you would get as many versions of that truth as there are relatives. Each of us sees things differently, through the lens of our experiences, biases, fears, and needs. The Thanksgiving scene—who arrived when, who sat where, the food, the conversation, and what caused that clatter in the kitchen—is now part of the past. The only means we have for resurrecting it are the memories of the humans who were there. Memory, therefore, is a representation (a *re*-presentation). Even if the whole thing had been recorded and watched on instant replay in the family room, we might know the *what* of what happened, but we still wouldn't know the *why* and the *how*. *Why* Uncle Rufus showed up late and *how* Mom felt when she heard him come through the door. *Why* Dad had a smirk on his face. *Why* cousin Iona grew silent. *How* Emmett felt as he sat there. *How*, when all was said and done, there was a pile of potatoes on the kitchen floor. Is anyone's conclusion on these matters more right or wrong than anyone else's? Not really.

Things are never exactly as they seem, in other words. The surrealist painter René Magritte sought to teach this by writing *"Ceci n'est pas une pipe" (This is not a pipe)* under his famous painting of a pipe, by which he meant: "This painting is not the same thing as the object that was painted." Think of memoir the same way: always one step removed from the experience it purports to depict. Moreover, we are biased either toward or against ourselves and others; we can't know what we do not know and often don't know why we did something, let alone what motivated someone else's behavior. And what we do know is, by definition, only what our memory has chosen to retain for us. Memoirists aim for accuracy, honesty, and fairness, knowing certainty is impossible to come by.

Since memoir covers a piece of a life rather than an entire life, a crucial consideration is whether the memories are ripe for the telling or should be allowed to age with time. Some memoirs are written during the thing itself, or right after. Some are written with the benefit of distance from the central events, which allows the memoirist to bring deeper wisdom and analysis to the story even at the expense of depleting memory.

For example, Frederick Douglass had a clear intention and an urgent need to write his memoir—*Narrative of the Life of Frederick Douglass, an American Slave*—shortly after securing his freedom, so he might draw further attention to slavery's cruelty and hasten its dissolution. From the start, he is aware of the memoir's potential for harm, too. Although he primes the reader to hear the harrowing tale of escape, in the end he explicitly states that he will not recount those details so as not to jeopardize the efforts of other slaves seeking freedom. His refusal to share what would no doubt have been the book's most compelling scene underscores for readers how much is at stake.

In *The Year of Magical Thinking*, Joan Didion endeavors to put emotional trauma under the microscope. She writes her memoir while fumbling through her own bewilderment in the immediate aftermath of her husband's death and her daughter's fight with a mysterious life-threatening illness. She chose to tap her emotions while they were fresh and raw so that she didn't lose them to memory. She aimed to capture the chaos of *right now* on the page so that the reader can come as close as possible to understanding what it *is* like to experience such things rather than offering a more analytical and dispassionate look at what it *was* like.

Cheryl Strayed took seventeen years to excavate meaning from the biggest events of her past. Her memoir, *Wild: From Lost to Found on the Pacific Crest Trail*, is, on the surface, about a grueling physical quest; on a deeper level, it's about her struggle to sort out her grief over her mother's death and her own serial betrayals and drug use, as well as to understand who she is, why she's done what she's done, and how she will make herself whole again.

Alison Bechdel waited twenty-six years after her father's suicide to write the graphic memoir *Fun Home: A Family Tragicomic*—enough time for the shame and bewilderment over her strange, emotionally controlled childhood to give way to understanding, empathy, and even kinship toward her profoundly flawed father.

Now it's your turn. Move to a desk and, with this book and a pencil or pen, summon the best memories you've got. The prompts herein will help you. Don't worry about the order of things, or how you'll link them together. Start by giving airtime to the memories that just won't quit—the ones that form the basis for your impulse to write memoir. Next, be curious about investigating the deeper story and harvest the best memories from conversations, interactions, events, experiences, inner feelings, and dreams. Press on your joy and moments of triumph and ask yourself why those times were so eventful—they are clues as to what matters most to you. Also press on what hurts in order to understand what you fear. The material you can't bear to face or write about could ultimately form some of your most impactful writing. See if you can go there. If you don't, you might make the mistake of telling the story that stands in front of the story that actually wants to be told. Dig up not just what happened to you but what you did to others. Tell yourself you can always take the hard bits out before anyone sees—for that is true—and it will also give you time to get comfortable seeing that stuff on the page.

If you're still struggling to pull back the facade, it's time to stand before a full-length mirror. Examine yourself. Readers want to see what is really there—warts and all—and to come to their own conclusions. Don't hold back. You've chosen to write memoir. You have to be okay with your flawed self, and all of the flawed selves in your story. You also have to be fair to everyone else. As my editor told me when I was writing my memoir, "Be the God of all characters," by which she meant care about everyone equally. Look at every interaction from all angles. Make sure you're not portraying yourself in rich complexity and everyone else as stereotype. My editor also meant I had to be realistic about myself. She told me, "Readers won't trust you or root for you unless they know about some of the stupid, shitty, and shameful things you have done." It felt like a paradox—*how are they going to like me if I give them a reason to hate me?* But I came to understand her point. All humans are flawed; a willingness to show your own flaws on the page makes you all the more relatable.

Memoirist Roxane Gay tests this theory in *Hunger*, in which she tells the story of her life prior to a rape at age twelve and her ensuing efforts to eat enough so that her body would be an impenetrable fortress. The brutality is evident, and the rapist's intentions are clear, so this memoir is not an effort to prove that what happened happened and that it was wrong. Instead, the stakes in this memoir are whether and how a trauma can have lasting impact over the course of a lifetime. Gay paints herself neither as flawless nor as certain. Right in the text, she second-guesses her memory and interpretation of it:

> I wish I could tell you I never spoke to Christopher [her rapist]
> again, but I did. That may be what shames me the most, that

after everything he did to me, I went back, and allowed him to continue using me until my family moved a few months later. I allowed him to continue using me because I didn't know what else to do. Or I let him use me because after what happened in the woods, I felt so worthless. I believed I didn't deserve any better.

She doubles back like this throughout the book, asserting something and then its opposite—

"I don't know how I let things get so out of control, but I do."
"I do not know why I turned to food. Or I do."
"I don't know why I'm telling you this. Or I do."
"I don't have anything to say to him, or rather, anything I would say to him. Or I do."

We are, in essence, watching Gay turn this way and that in the mirror. We trust her more because we see her struggle for a degree of clarity that eludes her. We know she's not offering us the best view of herself but simply the truest self she can locate and present to us. It makes her a hero. We champion Gay's sheer bravery and see it as an example of how we might be brave, too.

When learning to write memoir, I was taught that the best way to convey an experience is to "report from the body." The body senses what is happening before our brain interprets it and reveals information to us through things like sweaty palms, a dry mouth, or a rapidly beating heart. So, if you're still stuck in front of that mirror, close your eyes and recall a monumental experience. Can you remember how exactly your body signaled to you that something significant was going on? The body also serves as the repository of feeling and impact long after the pivotal moment has come and gone. In this passage from Douglass's memoir, we get a bodily sense of his suffering:

> I was seldom whipped by my old master, and suffered little from any thing else than hunger and cold. I suffered much from hunger, but much more from cold. In hottest summer and coldest winter, I was kept almost naked—no shoes, no stockings, no jacket, no trousers, nothing on but a coarse tow linen shirt, reaching only to my knees. I had no bed. I must have perished with cold, but that, the coldest nights, I used to steal a bag which was used for carrying corn to the mill. I would crawl into this bag, and there sleep on the cold, damp, clay floor, with my head in and feet out. My feet have been so cracked with the frost, that the pen with which I am writing might be laid in the gashes.

This could have been told with summary, such as "They were cruel. They didn't give us enough to eat, a place to sleep, or clothes to wear. It was desperately cold. My feet cracked from frost." Instead, we get a report that is visually compelling and becomes evidence of the literal scars of slavery borne by the body across decades. Douglass leaves us to our conclusions about what the treatment does to the mind.

Leaving readers to draw their own conclusions is extremely important in memoir. It's part of the trust equation. (If we tell our readers what to feel or think, they feel insulted, like we couldn't trust them to be along with us for the ride.) In *Angela's Ashes*, Frank McCourt's memoir of an impoverished childhood in Ireland, the author never lets his adult point of view or his adult judgments intrude on his child narrator self, who begins telling his tale at about age three. We never hear a screed about alcoholic fathers, birth control, or the persistence of poverty. He'd have certainly been within his rights had he chosen to rail against those things with all the power and might of his adult reasoning—and the result might have been strident, even polemical. Instead, he chose to illustrate these issues through the eyes of a suffering child for whom the reader feels nothing but compassion, and for that manner of telling, McCourt won the Pulitzer Prize.

Here's the sort of writing that earned McCourt the Pulitzer—this scene captures his six-year-old thoughts after his baby sister, Margaret, and twin brothers, Oliver and Eugene, die, all in a row:

> I don't know why we can't keep Eugene. I don't know why they have to send him away with that man who puts his pint on the white coffin. I don't know why they had to send Margaret away and Oliver. It is a bad thing to put my sister and my brothers in a box and I wish I could say something to someone.

McCourt stays true to what that six-year-old boy knew, thought, and could say at the time. He trusts that his readers can fill in all the gaps about cause, impact, and consequences. And of course, we can.

In this way, memoirists aren't so different from all storytellers. We have a responsibility to show more than we tell. To recall snappy, revealing dialogue that characterizes and moves plot at the same time. To convey humans who defy convention. To compel action and reaction and ripple effect and catharsis. To present the stakes (i.e., why any of this should *matter* to the reader). In essence, we have to be as good at all the basics as our novelist siblings, while walking a tightrope of trust and truth.

Inspired? Scared? Good. Move away from the mirror now, and sit back down. It's time. Give over to the inner plea: "Something happened to me and I think others should know about it." If this plea comes with the wild scream of ego needing attention, you might want to check yourself. (Memoir writing can be a wonderful catharsis, but do you need to inflict it on others? Maybe you just need to spend a lot of time writing in your journal.) Yet if the plea comes with quiet certainty that this topic bridges your human experience to that of others—sharpen your pencil. Humans yearn for connection, community, and meaning, and can find it in the well-told stories of others. Hold your primary readers close to your heart. If they know how tamales are made or how black hair should be handled, don't overexplain it; let those who don't get it look it up. Put differently, a good memoir is an act of service. The human condition in its alienation, pain, and joy yearns for a faithful scribe. Memoir offers readers that ultimate safe harbor: the knowledge that they are not alone.

....

Julie Lythcott-Haims is the *New York Times*–bestselling author of *How to Raise an Adult*. Her second book is the critically acclaimed and award-winning prose poetry memoir *Real American*. She holds a BA from Stanford, a JD from Harvard, and an MFA in Writing from California College of the Arts. She resides in the San Francisco Bay Area, where she is a member of the San Francisco Writers' Grotto.

writing memoir: a summary

- **Memoir is a true story.** Stay beholden to the truth, and write what in good conscience you truly believe you can recall. Acknowledge what you can't remember.

- **Know why you're writing it.** Write to be of use to others, not to make humans admire you.

- **Pick the right moment for this memoir.** During an ordeal? In the aftermath? Years later when events are more clearly understood? At the end of life?

- **Find the memories; they're the foundation for your writing.** You're panning for gold here. Sort them. Sift them. See what emerges.

- **Report from the body.** This is the best way to convey how something really felt. Again, don't summarize. Let the body tell it.

- **Earn the reader's trust.** Admit what you don't know. Admit when you were wrong. Admit the stupid thing you did. All of this will help the reader root for you.

- **Don't tell the reader what to think or feel.** Assume that all the good "showing" will allow the readers to form their own conclusions. They'll feel insulted if you tell them what to think or feel.

- **Remember the basics:** characterization, scene, setting, and dialogue.

writing prompts

just the facts, ma'am

Write a paragraph describing the life you currently lead in as factual a manner as possible.

Write it again, using the same facts, but creating a more pessimistic feel.

_____

_____

_____

_____

_____

_____

_____

Write it again, using the same facts, but creating a more optimistic feel.

_____

_____

_____

_____

_____

_____

_____

Imagine a memorable room in your life: the family kitchen, a bedroom, a garage. Make a list of every detail—the scents, the objects, the sounds—to make this room vivid.

enter a room

rosebud

From the list on the previous page, think of an object from your childhood, something that has strong associations or an emotional charge. Maybe a beloved doll, or the family car, or an ashtray, or a coaster that sat on the kitchen table.

How big was it, what color was it, how did it smell or feel in your hands?

_____

_____

_____

_____

_____

_____

If there is a person associated with it, describe the person. If there isn't a specific person, describe your family at the time the object was significant.

_____

_____

_____

_____

_____

_____

Think about why you remember it so vividly. Does it represent something about you or your life at that time? A sense of security or a painful awakening or a close relationship?

_____

_____

_____

_____

_____

Is there a story or scene or moment associated with the object that stands out to you most? Don't worry about outcome. Let the object lead you.

_____

_____

_____

_____

_____

Do the memories connect to anything in your current life? Is there something in this memory that feels relevant today?

_____

_____

_____

_____

_____

Write a list of words, phrases, or particular expressions that were common to your family or community. How many do you still use?

say what?

tour of the town

Now take your readers on a virtual tour of your hometown.
Begin at your front door and start walking. Narrate what
you see, what the weather is like, the sounds and smells you
encounter. Tell us about significant landmarks, either public
or personal.

what's the story?

What happens in your memoir?

_____

_____

_____

_____

_____

_____

_____

_____

_____

_____

_____

_____

_____

_____

_____

_____

_____

_____

_____

_____

_____

What's your memoir about? (The answer should not be the same as on the opposite page.)

_____

_____

_____

_____

_____

_____

_____

_____

_____

_____

_____

Despite what happens
in a memoir, the actual
message of the story
may be different. Your
memoir will contain
many facts and real-life
events, but they may not
accurately reflect the
idea you're trying to get
across. It's important to
both identify and distin-
guish between the two.

Write a list of words that were
used to describe you as a child,
whether by siblings, teachers, parents,
friends, strangers, or others.

jolly johnny

going home

Home is a state of mind as well as a place. Let the memories and associations of home—both good and bad—emerge. Were there times when home was a disappointment? Was there a specific time in your life when you felt most at home? What made you feel that way? Perhaps some of the words on the previous list even made you feel at home.

blind men and an elephant

Describe yourself from the point of view of the following people in your life:

The supermarket checker

_____

_____

_____

_____

_____

Your boss

_____

_____

_____

_____

_____

A child in your life

_____

_____

_____

_____

_____

Your next-door neighbor

_____

_____

_____

_____

_____

_____

Someone who works for you

_____

_____

_____

_____

_____

_____

A pet

_____

_____

_____

_____

_____

worth telling?

Tell a story about something from your private life that you're pretty sure no one cares to hear about. Just get it out of you!

_____

_____

_____

_____

_____

_____

_____

_____

_____

_____

_____

_____

_____

_____

_____

_____

_____

_____

_____

_____

question it

- Does someone need to read it to make you feel heard, or was writing it enough?

- Could you rewrite it in a way that would make readers care?

- Does it get at a larger truth?

- Could it be exactly what readers need from you in order to trust you?

Make a list of lies you've told, from
the small innocuous ones to whoppers
that changed the lives of others.

liar, liar

Write a list of secrets—ones you've
kept, ones you've betrayed, ones
you want to tell the world.

tell me a secret

it never happened

In one sentence, write down one of the secrets from the previous list that you think you could never publish.

_____

_____

_____

_____

_____

Write why you cannot publish it.

_____

_____

_____

_____

Then write why it's important to share it more widely.

_____

_____

_____

_____

And now do the same for one of the lies from page 37.

get moving

What is the physical movement or exercise that gives you the most pleasure and why? Write about being in the midst of that activity—your physical sensations, your thoughts, and your surroundings.

_____

_____

_____

_____

_____

_____

_____

_____

_____

_____

_____

_____

_____

_____

_____

_____

_____

_____

_____

over and over again

Think of a repeated event—the bus ride to school in fifth grade, Thanksgiving dinners at your aunt's house, piano lessons—and write down on the left all the details you remember. Who was there? What were you wearing? What did you or others say?

Now write down everything you don't remember. Sometimes what eludes memory can evoke the most powerful reflections.

your family as characters

Think of a member of your family you'd like to write about. Give them the kind of backstory a novelist would give a character.

What are their motivations?

_____

_____

_____

_____

_____

_____

_____

What are their disappointments?

_____

_____

_____

_____

_____

_____

_____

_____

_____

What are their struggles?

_____

_____

_____

_____

_____

How do they see you?

_____

_____

_____

_____

_____

How do they view their place in the family?

_____

_____

_____

_____

_____

What's in your purse or wallet?
List everything, right now.

gum in my wallet

you are your clutter

Describe a family member by the objects that you remember
seeing on their desk or dresser, or in their purse or wallet.

_____

_____

_____

_____

_____

_____

_____

_____

_____

_____

_____

_____

_____

_____

_____

_____

_____

_____

_____

Make a list of the unexpected things that make you happy. Be as specific as possible.

happy things

candy

Was candy on the previous list? Write about a memory of candy. Think about how much you wanted it, what color it was, how it made you feel, and where you were when you ate it. Was it the first time you'd ever had that candy before? What did it taste like? Was it your favorite candy?

fireworks on hot summer nights

Describe a memorable summer carnival or other celebration.
Maybe your sibling got lost in the crowd. Or you made out
for the first time. Or your parents got into a screaming match
at dinner. Read it over and try to come up with one word to
describe what this story is really about: the underlying theme.
Maybe it's loss or fear.

_____

_____

_____

_____

_____

_____

_____

_____

_____

_____

_____

_____

_____

_____

_____

_____

Now go back in and tweak what you wrote so this theme or idea or emotion is more manifest. Figure out "the thing you are really writing about when you are writing about something else" and turn the volume up on it. Let the particulars of the story lead you to its deeper meaning.

this is how it's done

Write, in detail, an instruction manual for something that you know how to do. It can either be something very specific (how to prune a rosebush) or something more abstract (how to survive a serious illness).

then and now

Write a scene from your life in the past tense.

Now write it again in the present tense, and notice how the
action changes.

a said, b said

Choose a moment of conflict or controversy. Write it from the perspective of one person.

_____

_____

_____

_____

_____

_____

_____

_____

_____

_____

_____

_____

_____

_____

_____

_____

_____

_____

_____

Now write it from the perspective of someone with a contrary opinion. Make them both compelling.

List twenty things you've wanted to accomplish in life. (Learn Spanish? Travel to Machu Picchu? Get a dog?) Now cross off those things you've already achieved.

bucket list

pivotal events

Zero in on the specific months or years that you want to focus on. Now list all the key events that happened during that time frame.

map it out

- Rewrite the list in chronological order.

- Circle the ten most pivotal events.

- Highlight the events you remember most vividly (i.e., the conversations, the details of the setting).

- Place check marks by the events that you know will be most controversial.

- Write out the event that will cause you the most pain to remember in detail.

self, meet self

Pick an upsetting incident from your past. Pretend that the person you were then goes to see a shrink who is also you, at any time or age you imagine. Have the shrink-self ask the patient-self a set of questions about the incident. Write that dialogue. See what you can reveal to the reader based upon the patient's inner thoughts and answers to the shrink.

Make a list of all the jobs you've
ever held, paid or unpaid.

working for a living

act your age!

Write a sentence describing an accident in the kitchen in the voice of a five-year-old.

_____

_____

_____

_____

_____

Write a sentence describing the same accident in the voice of a teenager.

_____

_____

_____

_____

_____

Write a sentence describing the same accident in the voice of a parent.

_____

_____

_____

_____

_____

Write a sentence of dialogue to go along with the accident—as spoken by a five-year-old.

_____

_____

_____

_____

_____

Write a sentence of dialogue to go along with the accident—as spoken by a teenager.

_____

_____

_____

_____

_____

Write a sentence of dialogue to go along with the accident—as spoken by a parent.

_____

_____

_____

_____

_____

some assembly required

Write about a time in which you had to assemble an object that required instructions with a partner. Tell the story of the relationship through or around the assembly. Consider doing this in the style or format of technical instructions.

show us how you feel

Recall an event of heightened emotion—fear, joy, sorrow, lust, envy, or shame, to name a few. Close your eyes and take yourself back to that moment; let yourself recall anything and everything about it. Then answer the following questions. The responses you come up with will provide sensory detail—imagery—to build the scene, making it real for the reader. Here's the kicker: Do *not* mention the emotion by name.

What do you see? What's up close? Far away?

_____

_____

_____

_____

_____

_____

What's the taste on your tongue? In the back of your mouth?

_____

_____

_____

_____

_____

_____

What do you hear? Far away and up close?

_____

_____

_____

_____

_____

What's against your skin? Where?

_____

_____

_____

_____

_____

What do you smell?

_____

_____

_____

_____

_____

kennedy, princess di, 9/11

Pick a historical event that happened in your lifetime. Write a scene with that as the backdrop as a way to tell us something significant about you.

_____

_____

_____

_____

_____

_____

_____

_____

_____

_____

_____

_____

_____

_____

_____

_____

_____

_____

Write a list of the things you're ashamed of
that also define you—a lie you told, a friend
you betrayed, a promise you didn't keep.

shame on me

_____ _____
_____ _____
_____ _____
_____ _____
_____ _____
_____ _____
_____ _____
_____ _____
_____ _____
_____ _____
_____ _____
_____ _____
_____ _____
_____ _____
_____ _____
_____ _____
_____ _____
_____ _____
_____ _____
_____ _____

a biography of your skin

Make a mental list of all the markings on your skin (past markings that have disappeared also count!). List tattoos, piercings, scars/wounds, birthmarks, vitiligo, unusual protuberances, any other visible or tactile variations, and perhaps the color itself. Pick three to five markings and write a paragraph about each. What is the story behind the mark?

or try this

- Create a montage essay of paragraphs that address different markings or aspects of your skin.

- Create a montage essay of paragraphs that each tell a different story about a singular mark.

- Pick one mark/one story and expand it into a full-length piece.

many voices, many masters

Recall a conversation held during a holiday meal or some other animated exchange with a lot of people. Write the scene, then use three different colors to highlight the three aspects of your own perspective that come into play: your id (what you said), your ego (what you really felt), and your superego (the internal voice that judges you). This exercise will illuminate the various facets of truth your character constantly wrestles with.

the body knows

The proverbial "Show, don't tell" can be exquisitely achieved by reporting from the body, drawing upon the five senses— sight, smell, sound, taste, and touch. Replace the following "tells" with a sentence or two each showing what the body experienced. Done well, the reader will come to the conclusion "she was afraid," "she was overjoyed," et cetera.

I am afraid. _____

_____

_____

_____

I'm overjoyed. _____

_____

_____

_____

I love it. _____

_____

_____

_____

I hate it. _____

_____

_____

_____

I'm in a hurry. _____

_____

_____

_____

_____

I couldn't care less. _____

_____

_____

_____

_____

I'm ashamed. _____

_____

_____

_____

_____

I'm mad. _____

_____

_____

_____

_____

List physical characteristics that define you, and how you and others have commented on them.

such a pretty face

let the reader decide

Summon a memory of a time in childhood when you felt misunderstood or mistreated. In a page, summarize the incident and then write a passionate defense of it in which you advocate to an authority figure about the fact that you were wronged.

_____

_____

_____

_____

_____

_____

_____

_____

_____

_____

_____

_____

_____

_____

_____

_____

_____

_____

Now write it again, but this time remove all of the advocacy and instead try to re-create all the details of the incident so you can show that you were wronged.

while it's hot (and cold)

Write up an incident that just happened to you while it's still fresh in your mind and your emotions are roiling. Describe the scene and the setting, what you did, and how you felt. Maybe you were cut off by another driver or waited over an hour for someone to show up (and received no apology!).

Now write up an emotionally charged incident that happened a while ago, at least six months. Describe the scene and the setting, what you did, and how you felt. Compare this writing to the facing page.

don't judge

What is the worst thing you've ever done? Describe the
moment or event in a neutral, fact-driven way, without
casting judgment on yourself.

Designer: Debbie Berne
Project Managers: Meghan Ward and Danielle Svetcov
Art Director: Diane Shaw
Editor: Meredith A. Clark
Production Manager: Rebecca Westall

ISBN: 978-1-4197-4138-8

Foreword © 2020 Julie Lythcott-Haims
Text © 2020 The Grotto, LLC
Cover © 2020 Abrams

Special thanks to: Beth Winegarner, Bonnie Tsui, Caroline Paul, Irving
Ruan, Jane Ciabattari, Julie Lythcott-Haims, Kristin Cosby, Laura Fraser,
Laura McClure, Lindsey Crittenden, Louise Nayer, Rachel Levin, Susan Ito,
Thaisa Frank, Zoe Fitzgerald Carter

Printed and bound in China

10 9 8 7 6 5 4 3 2 1

Abrams Noterie products are available at special discounts when purchased
in quantity for premiums and promotions as well as fundraising or educational
use. Special editions can also be created to specification. For details, contact
specialsales@abramsbooks.com or the address below.

ABRAMS The Art of Books
195 Broadway, New York, NY 10007
abramsbooks.com

MIX
Paper from
responsible sources
FSC™ C144853